# Legal Thrillers

## A Reader's Checklist And Reference Guide

The Original CheckerBee Checklist™

*The CheckerBee Checklist™ is not affiliated with or endorsed by any of the authors, publishers, publications or organizations referenced within.*

**CheckerBee Checklist™ is a trademark of CheckerBee, Inc.**

CheckerBee, Inc.
306 Industrial Park Road
Middletown, CT 06457
www.checklist.com



ISBN 1-58598-003-X

# Table Of Contents

## Table Of Contents

**Table Of Contents**

# Welcome To The World Of Legal Thrillers

There's nothing more thrilling than the twists and turns of a courtroom drama. Things are not always as they seem and the slightest detail can send any sort of order into pure chaos. The hero of the legal thriller is the attorney, usually one who is officially licensed to practice law, but sometimes one who is just thrust into the legal world as a result of some extraordinary circumstances. Regardless of the hero's occupation or the situation, legal thrillers allow readers to become part of the mystery, to see the clues and experience firsthand the unraveling of the events and possibly even solve the case for themselves. Because of this, the literary genre of legal thrillers has become one of the most popular and widely-read genres in the world today, proven by the number of such titles on best-seller lists as well as the success of those that have been adapted to the movie screen.

The **CheckerBee Checklist™** brings the exciting world of legal thrillers right to your fingertips with an easy-to-use system that will help you keep track of which books you've read and discover new books that you will want to read.

Fifty legal thriller novels have been selected for your reading pleasure. Narrowing down such a vast literary category to a list of only 50 proved difficult as, unfortunately, we could not include all of our favorite books and authors. We, however, hope to present a broad range of writers, cases and characters in the legal thriller genre for your enjoyment. Authors selected for inclusion in our checklist range from well-established authors in the genre (John Grisham, Scott Turow) to promising new authors (Lelia Kelly, Sabin Willett). And the book's characters represent attorneys with a large variety of legal expertise from civil litigation to criminal law – as well as some that never expected to find themselves in the middle of a legal predicament.

So, to help you plan your reading adventure, we've included the obvious and not-so-obvious, the best sellers and the yet-to-be-discovered gems.

The **CheckerBee Checklist™** includes detailed information about all the titles, highlighted by summaries of each book to help you pinpoint which ones you've read and to help you select your next book to read. Each page features room for you to record your personal reading history and you can even rate the books yourself! Other exciting features include biographies of all 50 featured authors, an overview of the prestigious awards that honor legal thriller authors and novels, a legal glossary of terms you will find throughout the genre and an easy-to-use checklist organized by lawyer type.

We hope that you will enjoy strolling through the 50 selected legal thrillers. You are sure to discover some wonderful new books, as well as find some new "favorite" authors. Maybe you'll even enjoy discussing the legal thriller titles you think should be featured in the next **CheckerBee Checklist™**. Happy reading!

# The History Of Legal Thrillers

Stories about law have been around for centuries. The quest for truth and justice has always fueled the matter of great stories. The judging of right and punishing of wrong is an ever-present human concern. But a new type of literary genre was formed when the drama of the courtroom was mixed with the action of the thriller; this genre became known as "legal thrillers."

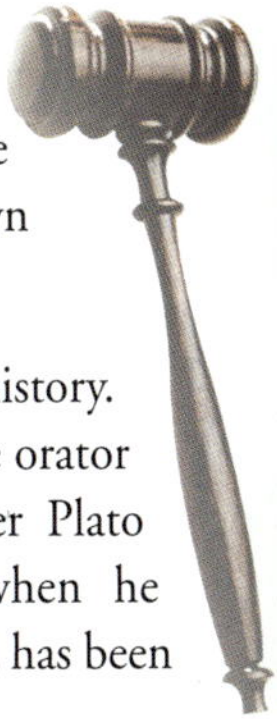

This genre's roots go way back through history. One cannot overlook the scholarly texts of the orator Cicero (106-43 B.C.). And the philosopher Plato wrote a courtroom drama, in a sense, when he chronicled the trial of Socrates. The law, then, has been a popular theme throughout the ages.

Courtroom drama saw its popularity start with the inspired novels of the hard-boiled writer Erle Stanley Gardner and the 1930s birth of his fictional litigator Perry Mason and Mason's popular sidekicks. Perry Mason was known for those dramatic court scenes in which a confession was wrenched out of a witness on the witness stand at the most critical point in the trial. This formulaic fiction made an easy transition to the television medium, with Raymond Burr immortalizing the famous sleuth, and the legal thriller genre's popularity was solidified.

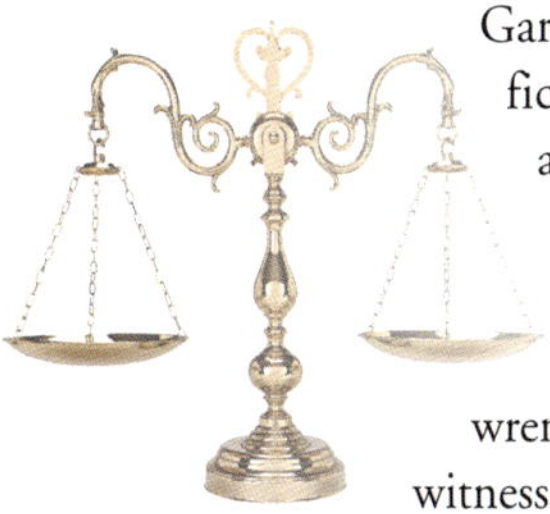

## The History Of Legal Thrillers

Another classic novel that brought courtroom drama to literary life is Harper Lee's Pulitzer Prize-winning book, *To Kill a Mockingbird* (1960). In this work, Lee told the story of a small-town lawyer defending a black man in the racial South. And the popularity of the genre was just not restricted to novels, for example, Agatha Christie's play *Witness for the Prosecution* (1953) is considered a classic of courtroom drama.

Novels that contained courtroom drama continued to capture the public's imagination. And these novels started to cover very controversial topics. With Robert Traver's *Anatomy of a Murder* (1958), topics such as rape that weren't discussed came out in the open, and the controversial film of the same name that was released in 1959 (with an older James Stewart playing the attorney) brought it to the attention of the nation.

The legal thriller barreled onto the popular literary scene in 1987 with the blockbuster success of Scott Turow's *Presumed Innocent*. The book tells the story of a former prosecutor who is now on trial himself for a murder, and who comes to realize the nebulous nature of justice. The book quickly became a best seller and a genre was, if not invented, then at least given new life. Prior to *Presumed Innocent*, those novels dealing with the workings of the law were generally classified as courtroom dramas.

However, with *Presumed Innocent*, the genre took a new turn. Turow went into greater detail about the actual trial mechanics – the intricacies of the attorney's strategies and the behind-the-scenes workings of the legal process – than ever before. And, while editors might have thought at first that readers would lose interest if legal technicalities were introduced into the story, they were wrong. Actually, readers crave this entertaining education in the world of law, and now many plots turn on such legal intricacies.

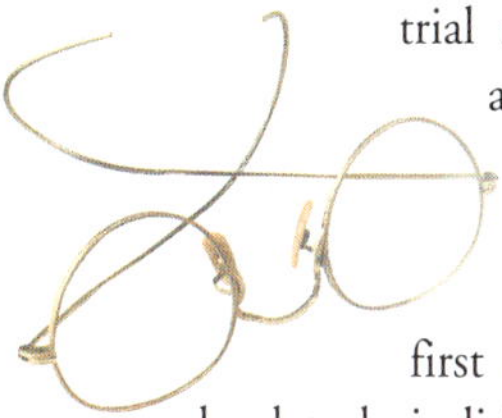

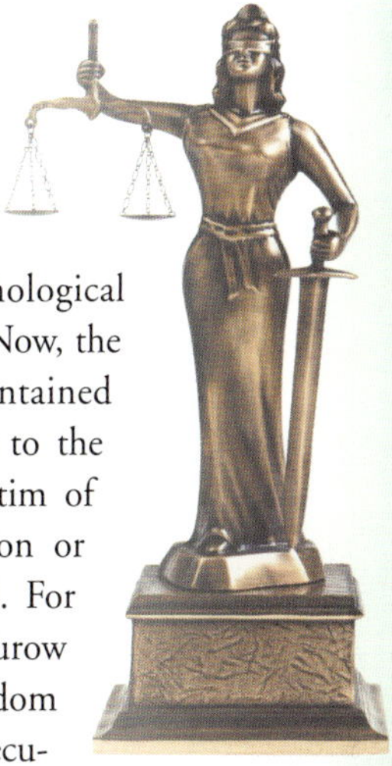

And new elements of high suspense and danger were also added which gave birth to the term legal "thriller." Thrillers, whether spy thrillers, technothrillers or psychological thrillers, have always been popular. Now, the drama of the courtroom also contained thriller aspects, like physical danger to the attorney, the attorney being the victim of political machinations and corruption or the attorney himself being put on trial. For example, in *Presumed Innocent*, Turow actually puts his protagonist's freedom and reputation in danger when prosecutor Rusty Sabich is put on trial for a murder he didn't commit. And the moral threat to Sabich is even greater, since it seems that someone in his own office is out to get him.

The popularity of the legal thriller, however, reached massive proportions with the success of a Southern lawyer named John Grisham. His first novel was *A Time to Kill* (1989), but Grisham really came into his own with *The Firm* (1991), whose film rights were bought before the manuscript was sold to a publisher. The story of a newly-made lawyer who unwittingly takes a job with a firm that launders money for the mob, this novel was devoured by readers from coast to coast, and spent an overwhelming 47 weeks on *The New York Times* best-seller list. And since Grisham is a very visual writer, his novels of legal plotting adapted well to the big screen and brought the genre to the attention of filmgoers everywhere. And casting the movie with the ever-popular Tom Cruise didn't hurt, either. This book, as well as subsequent novels such as *The Pelican Brief* (1992) and *The Client* (1993), would be the cement needed to fix Grisham's place as the king of the genre, as well as guarantee the popularity of legal thrillers for years to come.

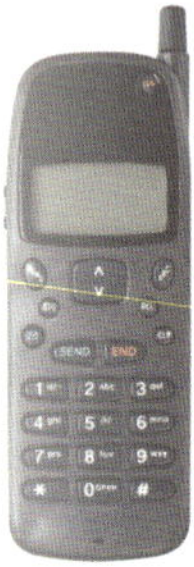

Men are not the only authors of legal thrillers. Women are also prominent writers in the legal thriller genre, and many books feature female attorneys as the main character. Lisa Scottoline, who's been called "the female John Grisham" by *People*, writes novels containing female protagonists. Carolyn Wheat has a whole series dedicated to her Brooklyn litigator Cass Jameson, while Lia Matera bases her books around San Francisco attorney Laura Di Palma. So it's no longer the "old boys club" that the legal profession once was!

But, thriller aspects aside, what exactly is the appeal of this genre? The fact that most of the authors are, or have been, attorneys and really "know their stuff" is certainly a factor. This realism adds to the validity and the dramatic verve of the fiction. The attorney, or judge, turned novelist is the most common producer of the legal thriller, although people from other backgrounds have gotten into the act as well. Sarah Caudwell, Phillip Margolin and Barbara Parker are just a few of the authors who have turned their personal experiences and unique insight as attorneys into suspenseful and gripping novels. They know firsthand the conflicts, tension and ethical dilemmas that are part of the attorney's everyday life.

The allure of the legal thriller also stems from the ubiquitous nature of lawyers, trials and lawsuits in modern life, as we turn to the courts more and more to make decisions that used to be settled by other societal institutions. Perhaps most of all, it is the timelessness and universal notions of the courtroom drama – where the age-old pursuit of truth and justice, and the struggle for good to triumph over evil are played out – that have the power to hold us rapt. All of these elements, combined with the action, mystery and often romance that are present in most legal thrillers, make it easy to understand its appeal.

And most times the main plot is paralleled by a story line of the main character's personal crisis. So although most of us will never find ourselves on the run from mobsters or the government because we know too much about

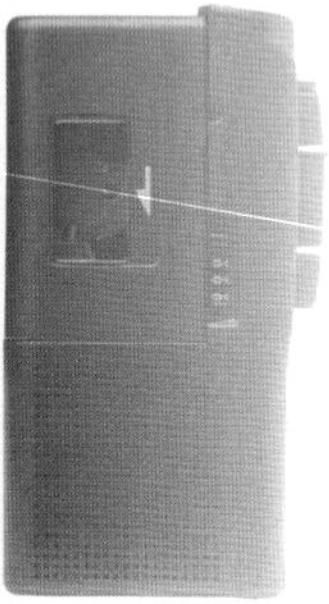

some shady dealing, or be in the position of having to defend a serial killer or some other unsavory person, we can still relate to the central issues and characters in these books, while, at the same time, taking an escapist roller-coaster ride through unfamiliar terrain.

Legal thrillers have flooded the market, supplying the rising demand from a public that can't get enough of courtroom intrigue, suspense and the quest for justice. There is a deluge of all things legal in every area of entertainment – just look at the popularity of such TV shows such as *Law & Order* and *The Practice*. Court TV, Judge Judy, and the O.J. Simpson trial, also have brought legalese into the living room. Even President Clinton's impeachment trial brought more intricacies of the legal system to the American consciousness.

Every legal thriller is different and each writer has his or her own voice and views. Some of the books listed in this checklist are humorous, some are dark and noirish, some feature down-on-their-luck underdogs and others, successful corporate attorneys. All will hold you enthralled and take you into a world that has been reviled by some and romanticized by others – the world of the law, where numerous dramas are played out every day.

# How To Use Your CheckerBee Checklist™

## It's A Checklist *and* A Reference Guide!

The **CheckerBee Checklist™** is an easy-to-use guide to some of your favorite legal thriller novels! The guide is filled with 50 great novels, all arranged alphabetically according to author, from Baldacci to Woods. Each entry contains the **publication date**, the **publisher** and the **page count** of the first edition. As some of the titles are printed in various formats by different publishers, page counts may vary.

Following the publishing information, we've provided the **setting, lawyer type** and a **plot summary** for each title. The **CheckerBee Checklist™** also features ***The New York Times*** **best-seller rankings**, prominent book **awards,** selected **book reviews** and **movie information**. In addition to all of this, many of the titles have a **CheckerBee Note** which provides an interesting tidbit of information about the work. The book reviews are from various respected publications, such as *Publishers Weekly* and *Kirkus Reviews*, and the awards are given by prominent trade publications and organizations. If a particular title has been adapted into a movie, the year of release and the main cast are listed.

The checklist also has icons for the various **publishing formats** in which each title is available. The five icons represent *hardcover*, *paperback*, *large print*, *audio* and *video editions*. On each page, only the icons applicable to that particular title will appear. Keep in mind that some of these editions may now be "out of print," which means they may be difficult to track down through traditional bookstores.

## Record Your Personal Reading History!

You can check off the "Want to Read" box to plan your future reading list. Check boxes also appear next to the movie information and the publishing formats, so you can keep track of which versions you own or which versions you've read, listened to or watched. In the **Date Read** section, you can record the date you read the book. You can also rate each book on a scale from one to five stars in the **My Rating** section and put notes in the **My Comments** section.

You can also track what you've read with a checklist organized by **Lawyer Type** in the back of the book and the **Reader's Notes** section on page 93 allows you to keep notes about your reading adventure.

### Icon Key

| | | |
|---|---|---|
| MOVIE Motion Picture | Hard COVER Hardcover | Audio Audio |
| TV MOVIE Television Movie | PAPER BACK Paperback | Video Video |
| | LARGE PRINT Large Print | |

# Absolute Power
## by David Baldacci

☐ Want to Read

*1996 • Warner Books • 480 pages*

New York Times #2
17 Weeks On List

**Setting:** Middleton, Virginia and Washington, D.C., 1990s
**Type:** Corporate attorney

Aging burglar Luther Whitney has found an irresistible job: burglarizing the mansion of a Virginia billionaire. Things go awry when the billionaire's wife arrives home with her lover, who is none other than the President of the United States. Luther hides and ends up witnessing the violent murder of the president's mistress. Now, with a key piece of evidence in hand, Luther is on the run, with only Attorney Jack Graham to help him, and the chilling realization that the president's inner circle will stop at nothing to conceal the truth.

"... sizzler of a first novel ..."
*–Publishers Weekly*

☐ MOVIE (1997) starring Clint Eastwood and Gene Hackman

☐ Hard COVER ☐ PAPER BACK ☐ LARGE PRINT ☐ Audio ☐ Video

☐ Date Read: ____________ My Rating (circle): ★ ★ ★ ★ ★

My Comments: ______________________________

# Perfect Justice
## by William Bernhardt

☐ Want to Read

*1994 • Ballantine Books • 384 pages*

**Setting:** Silver Springs, Arkansas, 1990s
**Type:** Criminal defense attorney

When Oklahoma attorney Ben Kincaid travels to Arkansas on vacation, he finds the town of Silver Springs boiling over with racial tension. A Vietnamese boy has been killed and all fingers point to Donald Vick, a member of a hate group called the ASP (Anglo-Saxon Patrol). Kincaid, who believes that all people deserve representation, decides to defend Vick. The town soon closes ranks against Kincaid and his client tells him to plead him guilty. But the most shocking thing of all to Kincaid is that his client may actually be innocent!

### Awards

1995 Oklahoma Book Award winner for Best Fiction

### CheckerBee Note

This is the 4th in a series of novels featuring Ben Kincaid.

☐ Hard COVER ☐ PAPER BACK ☐ LARGE PRINT ☐ Audio

☐ Date Read: ________ My Rating (circle): ★ ★ ★ ★ ★

My Comments: ________________

# Prejudicial Error
## by Bill Blum

☐ Want to Read

*1995 • Dutton • 289 pages*

**Setting:** Los Angeles, 1990s
**Type:** Criminal defense attorney

John Solomon lost his promising career as chief trial deputy in the Los Angeles D.A.'s office after his affair came to light. Now, trying petty cases and losing himself in drink, Solomon is given a chance to redeem himself by defending an accused cop-killer, Juan Thomas. All is not as it seems, though, as Solomon learns that he's been picked because he's certain to lose the case. The more he probes, the more it appears that Thomas may have been set up, and that the real criminals lurk within the LAPD and the district attorney's office itself.

". . . a well-constructed thriller from a writer to watch."
*–Publishers Weekly*

☐ Hard COVER ☐ PAPER BACK

☐ Date Read: ____________ My Rating (circle): ★ ★ ★ ★ ★

My Comments: ______________________________

# Local Rules
## by Jay Brandon

☐ Want to Read

*1995 • Pocket Books • 290 pages*

**Setting:** Green Hills, Texas, 1990s
**Type:** Criminal defense attorney

San Antonio attorney Jordan Marshall is on his way to a day at the beach when he is pulled over for speeding in the small town of Green Hills. The local judge offers him a deal – he'll drop the speeding ticket if Jordan will represent Wayne Orkney, a local teenager accused of the attempted murder of his best friend, Kevin Wainwright. Jordan agrees after being assured that it should be a quick plea, but he soon realizes that there is more behind the case when the prosecution calls for a rather severe sentence. When Kevin Wainwright dies in the hospital, the charge becomes murder. As Jordan digs deeper, he uncovers some small-town secrets that aren't so small.

☐ Hard COVER ☐ PAPER BACK ☐ LARGE PRINT ☐ Audio

☐ Date Read: ________ My Rating (circle): ★ ★ ★ ★ ★

My Comments:

# The Defense
## by D.W. Buffa

☐ Want to Read

*1997 • Henry Holt and Company, Inc.*
*224 pages*

**Setting:** Oregon, 1990s
**Type:** Criminal defense attorney

Joseph Antonelli is a win-at-all-costs defense attorney whose ethics have never conflicted with his perfect trial record. So it's business as usual when his friend and mentor, Judge Rifkin, asks him for a favor – defend Johnny Morel, a drug dealer accused of raping his 12-year-old stepdaughter. Despite overwhelming evidence against Morel, Antonelli gets him acquitted. The subsequent murders of both the rapist and the girl's mother, and implications of Rifkin's possible involvement, will lead Antonelli to the trial of his career, while forcing into question everything he believes about the legal system.

"... an ingenious, riveting legal thriller ..."
*–Publishers Weekly*

☐ Hard COVER ☐ PAPER BACK ☐ Audio

☐ Date Read: ________ My Rating (circle): ★ ★ ★ ★ ★

My Comments: ________

# Thus Was Adonis Murdered
## by Sarah Caudwell

Want to Read

*1981 • Scribner • 246 pages*

**Setting:** Venice, Italy and London, 1980s
**Type:** Barrister

In this intelligent and witty British mystery, a group of young barristers and Hilary Tamar, an Oxford law professor, come to the aid of their friend Julia Larwood, a barrister without much common sense. Never really believing that she had to pay taxes, Julia has let years go by without filing a tax return. When Inland Revenue finds out and demands back taxes, Julia is stressed, indeed. So she decides to go on a holiday in Venice, where she takes up with a handsome young man, who also happens to be an employee of Inland Revenue. And when he turns up dead in her bed, Julia's in hot water. It's now up to Julia and her friends to prove her innocence.

"An elaborately plotted, very English and charming story."
*–Kirkus Reviews*

Hard COVER PAPER BACK

Date Read: ________ My Rating (circle): ★ ★ ★ ★ ★

My Comments: ________

# Shadow of a Doubt
## by William J. Coughlin

☐ Want to Read

*1991 • St. Martin's Press • 390 pages*

**Setting:** Pickeral Point, Michigan, 1990s
**Type:** Criminal defense attorney

Once a high-profile lawyer, Charley Sloan was nearly disbarred because of his drinking problem. But when an old flame, Robin Harwell, returns to ask him to defend her stepdaughter Angel against charges that she murdered her millionaire father Harrison, he takes the challenge in hopes of redeeming himself. This proves increasingly difficult as the evidence mounts, including an apparent confession and the discovery of Angel's fingerprints on the knife. Charley must now untangle the string of lies and get to the truth – who really killed Harrison Harwell?

"Seldom does mystery/thriller fiction ring as true as this lucid, emotionally demanding book."
*–Publishers Weekly*

☐ TV MOVIE (1995) starring Brian Dennehy, Bonnie Bedelia and Fairuza Balk

☐ Hard COVER ☐ PAPER BACK ☐ LARGE PRINT

☐ Date Read: ________ My Rating (circle): ★ ★ ★ ★ ★

My Comments: ________

# Tainted Evidence

## by Robert Daley

Want to Read

*1993 • Little, Brown and Company • 391 pages*

**Setting:** New York City, 1990s
**Type:** Assistant district attorney

Racial tensions threaten to boil over when a black murder suspect Lionel Epps shoots five cops during a police raid. Caught in the middle of this turmoil is Assistant D.A. Karen Henning, who has been assigned to the case. The defendant's lawyer, Justin McCarthy, is a well-known civil rights lawyer who is ready and willing to use these racial tensions to help his case. As the drama spirals out of the courts and into the public eye, the very system that Henning has fought so hard to uphold is threatening to crumble at her feet.

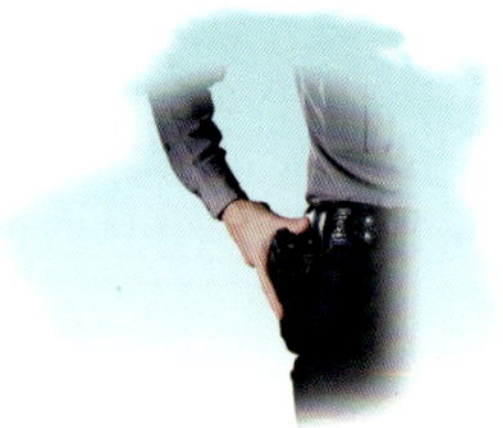

"Steadily gripping . . . No one does it better."
*–Kirkus Reviews*

MOVIE *Night Falls on Manhattan* (1997) starring Andy Garcia and Richard Dreyfuss

Hard COVER | PAPER BACK | LARGE PRINT | Audio | Video

Date Read: ________ My Rating (circle): ★ ★ ★ ★ ★

My Comments:

# Primal Fear
## by William Diehl

Want to Read

*1993 • Villard Books • 418 pages*

**Setting:** Chicago, 1983
**Type:** Criminal defense attorney

A highly-respected archbishop, known as "the Saint of Lakeview Drive," is brutally murdered in his rectory, with altar boy Aaron Stampler, bloodied and holding the murder weapon, found just feet away from the crime scene in the church's confessional. Chicago attorney Martin Vail is defending Stampler in what seems to be an open-and-shut case. But Vail soon finds himself deep into an investigation which reveals one shocking secret after another. For starters, Stampler may indeed be innocent, and it seems the archbishop was no saint after all.

"Shocking . . . As much psychological thriller as legal drama . . . Diehl delivers."
*–People*

☐ MOVIE (1996) starring Richard Gere and Edward Norton

☐ Hard COVER ☐ PAPER BACK ☐ Audio ☐ Video

☐ Date Read: ________ My Rating (circle): ★ ★ ★ ★ ★

My Comments: ____________________

# Brain Storm
## by Richard Dooling

Want to Read

*1998 • Random House • 416 pages*

**Setting:** St. Louis, 2002
**Type:** Legal researcher

Joe Watson is leading a charmed life, with a cushy research job for a prestigious St. Louis law firm, which hardly ever requires him to step inside a courtroom. But when a judge appoints Joe to a defend a federal murder case with the accused to be prosecuted under the new hate crime statutes (the victim was a deaf, black man), his life takes an unforeseen turn. His wife and his boss have definite plans for his actions and he risks losing both his family and his job if he doesn't comply. With a zany cast of characters, including a sexy neuroscientist and a "punk rock" criminal defense attorney, Joe plans to become the best criminal defense lawyer he can be.

"His passion for the law pulls us breathlessly along."
*–Booklist*

Hard COVER PAPER BACK Audio

Date Read: ________ My Rating (circle): ★ ★ ★ ★ ★

My Comments: ________

# Witness for the Defense

## by Michael C. Eberhardt

☐ Want to Read

*1998 • Onyx • 416 pages*

**Setting:** San Francisco, 1990s
**Type:** Public defender

Hunter Dobbs, a dedicated public defender has just been accused of coercing testimony from a witness and now the California Bar is investigating. Sarah Harris, a fellow lawyer and the daughter of a judge with whom Dobbs has always been at odds, offers to represent Hunter if he will reciprocate. She wants him to represent a family friend who is accused of kidnapping and molesting a young boy. Then a murder occurs and the entire foundation of the justice system seems to be up in the air.

☐ PAPER BACK

☐ Date Read: ________ My Rating (circle): ★ ★ ★ ★ ★

My Comments: ____________________

____________________

____________________

____________________

# Final Jeopardy
## by Linda Fairstein

Want to Read

*1996 • Scribner Book Co. • 400 pages*

**Setting:** New York City and Martha's Vineyard, Massachusetts, 1990s
**Type:** Assistant district attorney

As Manhattan's Assistant D.A. in charge of sex crimes, Alexandra Cooper thought she had seen everything. But nothing could have prepared her for the shock of reading her own obituary in the *New York Post*, describing her as the victim of a brutal murder. The actual victim was film star Isabella Lascar, who had been staying at Alex's Martha's Vineyard retreat. Had the killer mistaken her for Alex, or had a crazed stalker traced Isabella to the island? If the killer is after her, Alex has an endless list of suspects, but time is running out and she must find the killer before he finds her.

"... [An] exciting first novel ... a memorable debut."
*–Publishers Weekly*

☐ Hard COVER ☐ PAPER BACK ☐ LARGE PRINT ☐ Audio

☐ Date Read: __________ My Rating (circle): ★ ★ ★ ★ ★

My Comments: ______________________________

# Tell Me No Secrets
## by Joy Fielding

☐ Want to Read

*1993 • William Morrow and Company, Inc.*
*352 pages*

**Setting:** Chicago, 1990s
**Type:** District attorney

Successful district attorney Jess Kostner is being stalked. Kostner is in the middle of prosecuting Rick Ferguson for rape charges against Connie DeVuono when Connie vanishes and Jess begins to receive death threats. As Kostner hasn't exactly surrounded herself with men she can trust, there are many possible stalkers. Is it her flirtatious, married colleague, her ex-husband, her secretive new boyfriend or the rapist she's trying to prosecute? Or is it none of the above? Whomever it is, Jess must find out fast before she winds up dead!

". . . an ingeniously crafted finale . . ."
*–Publishers Weekly*

☐ TV MOVIE (1997) starring Lori Loughlin and Bruce Greenwood

☐ Hard COVER ☐ PAPER BACK ☐ LARGE PRINT ☐ Audio

☐ Date Read: ________ My Rating (circle): ★ ★ ★ ★ ★

My Comments: ____________________

# High Crimes
## by Joseph Finder

☐ Want to Read

*1998 • William Morrow and Company, Inc.*
*352 pages*

**Setting:** Boston, Washington, D.C. and Quantico, Virginia, 1990s
**Type:** Law professor and criminal defense attorney

Harvard law professor Claire Heller Chapman is devastated when she finds out that her husband Tom is really Ron Kubik, a former Pentagon operative who is wanted for the murder of 87 civilians in El Salvador. He has changed his name and his face – and everything Claire knew about his past was a lie. Now he has been arrested by federal agents and is to be tried in a top-secret court-martial. Tom swears that he is innocent and Claire takes on his defense. Can she prove her husband's innocence, even when she's not so sure of it herself?

### CheckerBee Note

The film rights to this novel were sold to Tri-Star Pictures.

☐ Hard COVER ☐ PAPER BACK ☐ Audio

☐ Date Read: ________ My Rating (circle): ★ ★ ★ ★ ★

My Comments: ________________

# Against the Wind
## by J.F. Freedman

☐ Want to Read

*1991 • Viking • 423 pages*

**Setting:** Santa Fe, New Mexico, 1990s
**Type:** Criminal defense attorney

Will Alexander's life is crumbling. His wife is about to leave him and he's about to be asked to leave his firm. But, things brighten a little when a case falls his way. A chance to salvage his soiled reputation is offered when he agrees to defend four outlaw bikers who are accused of mutilating and murdering a local drug dealer. He believes that his clients are innocent, that they were too busy with other pursuits on the night of the murder. Months later, more evidence turns up and the prosecution's lead witness admits to perjury. Now, Will must widen his investigation to discover the truth.

"... one of the most extravagantly entertaining thrillers of the year."
*–Kirkus Reviews*

☐ Hard COVER ☐ PAPER BACK ☐ Audio

☐ Date Read: ________ My Rating (circle): ★ ★ ★ ★ ★

My Comments: ________________________________

________________________________________________

________________________________________________

________________________________________________

# Reasonable Doubt
## by Philip Friedman

Want to Read

*1990 • Donald I. Fine, Inc. • 487 pages*

**Setting:** New York City, 1990s
**Type:** Criminal defense attorney

Michael Ryan, an ex-federal prosecutor, hasn't seen his son Ned in the years since Ned publicly accused his father of being responsible for his mother's death. Now, Michael has just learned of Ned's death – he was beaten to death in a room of a Soho art gallery. Ned's wife, Jennifer Kneeland Ryan, has been accused of the murder and Michael hesitantly agrees to defend her, even though he doesn't believe she's innocent. Before the truth can come out, Ryan must discover some unsavory details about his son, as well as confront his own past.

". . . as crisply written and ingeniously plotted a courtroom entertainment as readers are apt to encounter this side of the county courthouse."
*–Entertainment Weekly*

Hard COVER  PAPER BACK

Date Read: ________ My Rating (circle): ★ ★ ★ ★ ★

My Comments: ________

# Reckless Homicide
## by Ira Genberg

☐ Want to Read

*1998 • St. Martin's Press • 304 pages*

**Setting:** Washington, D.C., 1990s
**Type:** Corporate attorney

When Michael Ashmore, chief counsel for Brandon Air Lines, helps conceal his pilot brother Charlie's failed drug test results, he puts himself in a world of trouble. When Charlie's plane goes down – killing all on board – and an autopsy reveals barbiturates in Charlie's system, Ashmore must fight to redeem his brother's name and his own career.

"Genberg brilliantly breathes new life into . . . [the] genre . . . The sort of twist-your-guts stuff that catapults *Reckless Homicide* into the must-read category."
–*The Atlanta Journal-Constitution*

☐ Hard COVER ☐ PAPER BACK

☐ Date Read: ____________ My Rating (circle): ★ ★ ★ ★ ★

My Comments: ______________________________

# The Pardon
## by James Grippando

☐ Want to Read

*1994 • HarperCollins • 320 pages*

**Setting:** Florida, 1994
**Type:** Criminal defense attorney

When Jack Swyteck had attempted to get a stay of execution for a client, the governor of Florida (and Jack's estranged father) Harry Swyteck refused the request. At the time, Jack had claimed to have proof of his client's innocence, but his claim was ignored. Now someone is bent on revenge against both Harry and Jack, with the ultimate goal of pinning a murder on Jack. Could it be the "Chrysanthemum Killer?" In a surprising turn of events, Jack's innocence must be proven before Harry is forced to sign his own son's death warrant.

"A gritty mystery that . . . rings true to the emotional realities of contemporary life. Readers will turn the pages of 'The Pardon' faster than a bailiff can swear in a witness."
*–People*

☐ Hard COVER ☐ PAPER BACK ☐ LARGE PRINT ☐ Audio

☐ Date Read: ____________ My Rating (circle): ★ ★ ★ ★ ★

My Comments: ____________________

# The Firm
## by John Grisham

☐ Want to Read

*1991 • Doubleday • 432 pages*

New York Times #2
47 Weeks On List

**Setting:** Memphis, Tennessee and the Cayman Islands, 1990s
**Type:** Corporate attorney

Mitch McDeere has graduated at the top of his class from Harvard Law School and can join any firm he wants. He chooses to accept a job with a small but well-respected tax firm in Memphis, complete with unbelievable benefits. But strange things are happening and McDeere discovers that his firm is run by a very powerful organized crime ring. Now the FBI wants him as an informant, but the firm has other plans for him.

"Keeps the reader hooked . . . From the creepy first chapters . . . to the vise-tightening midsection and on to the take-the money-and-run finale."
*–The Wall Street Journal*

☐ MOVIE (1993) starring Tom Cruise, Holly Hunter, Jeanne Tripplehorn and Gene Hackman

☐ Hard COVER ☐ PAPER BACK ☐ LARGE PRINT ☐ Audio ☐ Video

☐ Date Read: ____________ My Rating (circle): ★ ★ ★ ★ ★

My Comments: ______________________________

# Fatal Reaction
## by Gini Hartzmark

Want to Read

*1998 • Ivy Books • 352 pages*

**Setting:** Chicago, 1990s
**Type:** Corporate attorney

When the lawyer for Azor Pharmaceuticals is brutally murdered in the midst of a large deal with a Japanese drug company, the head of Azor, Stephen Azorini, asks his girlfriend and attorney Kate Millholland to complete the deal. She takes over the negotiations, but vows to find out who Danny's killer was. The case is baffling and raises many questions. For example, Danny and his apartment were covered in blood, but there wasn't a cut on him. And did the fact that Danny was gay and HIV positive have something to do with his death? The answers will lead Kate to secrets about everyone involved and to some deadly drug-experimenting practices.

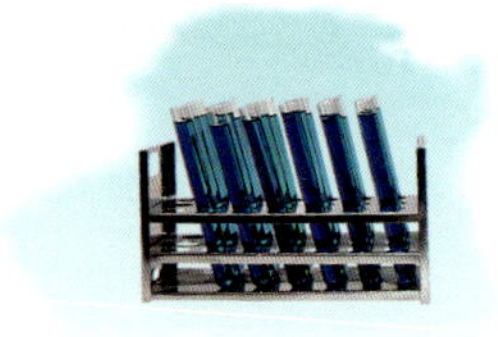

**CheckerBee Note**

This is Hartzmark's 4th novel to feature Kate Millholland.

PAPER BACK

Date Read: ________ My Rating (circle): ★ ★ ★ ★ ★

My Comments: ________

# Sheer Gall
## by Michael A. Kahn

Want to Read

*1996 • Dutton • 308 pages*

**Setting:** St. Louis, 1990s
**Type:** Civil litigator

Sally Wade appears in attorney Rachel Gold's office, bruised and battered, and claiming that her soon-to-be ex-husband Neville, a pillar of the community, is responsible. Wade wants to sue him for assault and Gold eagerly accepts the case. When Sally is murdered before the case goes to court, Rachel naturally suspects that her client's husband is the culprit. The plot thickens, however, when Neville's slick defense attorney raises doubts in Rachel's mind over Neville's guilt, and suggests that the woman who appeared in Gold's office may have been an imposter. Rachel sets out to find the truth, and uncover a killer.

### CheckerBee Note

This is Kahn's 5th novel to feature attorney Rachel Gold.

☐ Hard COVER ☐ PAPER BACK

☐ Date Read: __________ My Rating (circle): ★ ★ ★ ★ ★

My Comments: ______________________________

# Hart's War
## by John Katzenbach

☐ Want to Read

*1999 • Ballantine Books • 496 pages*

**Setting:** Germany, 1940s
**Type:** Law student

Second Lieutenant Tommy Hart has been a prisoner in Stalag Luft 13, a German prisoner-of-war camp, since 1942 when his B-25 bomber was shot down. To pass the time, he keeps up with his law studies which had been interrupted with the outbreak of the war. Tommy gets a chance to use his legal skills when he is appointed to defend First Lieutenant Lincoln Scott, an African-American Tuskegee airman who has been accused of killing a racist fellow prisoner. As the trial seems nothing more than a formality, Tommy must cut through the racial hatred and secret motives to get to the truth.

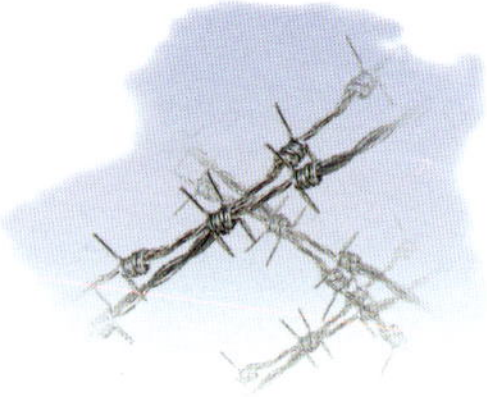

". . . this deeply affecting, artfully paced war epic will hold readers enthralled to the nail-biting end."
*–Publishers Weekly*

☐ **Hard** COVER

☐ Date Read: ______ My Rating (circle): ★ ★ ★ ★ ★

My Comments: ______

# Presumption of Guilt
## by Lelia Kelly

Want to Read

*1998 • Kensington • 231 pages*

**Setting:** Atlanta, 1990s
**Type:** Criminal defense attorney

When Atlanta lawyer Laura Chastain agrees to defend a white cop accused of killing a black suspect while he was being held in custody, she knows she's going headlong into a controversial, racially-heated case. Still, there's more to the case than even Chastain suspected. The accused cop, Detective Jeff Williams, believes he is being set up by his fellow officers. If he's right, both of their lives could be in danger, as Chastain's investigation takes her into a web of lies, deceit and murder.

"Vivid and involving."
*–Booklist*

Hard COVER  PAPER BACK

Date Read: ________ My Rating (circle): ★ ★ ★ ★ ★

My Comments: ________

# The 13th Juror
## by John T. Lescroart

☐ Want to Read

*1994 • Donald I. Fine, Inc. • 484 pages*

**Setting:** San Francisco, 1990s
**Type:** Criminal defense attorney

Defense attorney Dismas "Diz" Hardy has taken on the case of Jennifer Lee Witt, a woman accused of killing her husband and young son. Yet Hardy's client, a battered wife, is less than cooperative – refusing to use marital violence in her defense. And to make matters worse, the prosecutors attempt to prove that Witt had also killed her previous husband. Will Witt be willing to take the risk of revealing the truth about her marriage in order to prove her innocence?

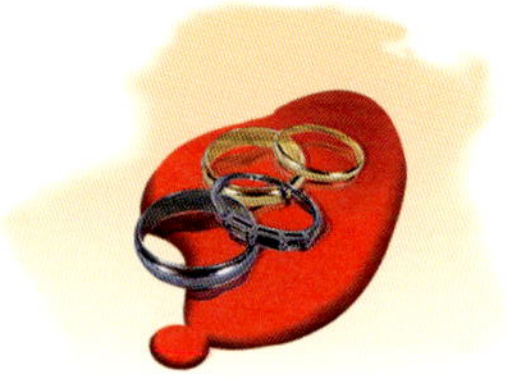

". . . a fast-paced text that sustains interest to the very end."
*–The Wall Street Journal*

☐ Hard COVER ☐ PAPER BACK ☐ LARGE PRINT ☐ Audio

☐ Date Read: ________ My Rating (circle): ★ ★ ★ ★ ★

My Comments: ______________________

# Night Vision
## by Paul Levine

☐ Want to Read

*1991 • Bantam Books • 342 pages*

**Setting:** Miami and London, 1990s
**Type:** Special prosecutor

Jake Lassiter, a former Miami Dolphins linebacker and now a lawyer, has been appointed as the special prosecutor in a murder case. The victim was Michelle Diamond, a TV newscaster who was found strangled. There are several possible suspects, including D.A. Nick Wolf, who was Michelle's lover and who may be covering up shady happenings he was involved with during his tour of duty in Vietnam, and the owners of Compu-Mate, a computer sex line that Michelle frequented. As more bodies surface, the urgency of the situation increases. It is up to Jake to find and stop this serial killer.

### CheckerBee Note

Jake Lassiter was introduced to readers in Levine's debut novel, *To Speak for the Dead.*

☐ Hard COVER ☐ PAPER BACK

☐ Date Read: ________ My Rating (circle): ★ ★ ★ ★ ★

My Comments: ____________________

# Chain of Custody
## by Harry Levy

Want to Read

*1998 • Random House • 304 pages*

**Setting:** New York City, 1990s
**Type:** Medical malpractice litigator

Dr. Michael Malone, a cardiologist and police surgeon-turned-lawyer, is being accused of his wife's murder and the cards are pretty well stacked against him. First, his medical background provides him with the knowledge of how to cover up his deeds. Also, his blood has been found at the crime scene and his wife's blood been found on his belongings. The fact that the Malones were in the middle of a bitter divorce and he stood a chance of losing custody of his son doesn't help his case. Michael knows he's innocent and it's apparent that he's being framed. Can he discover the truth before it's too late?

"Levy's effort generates real tension and boasts a fascinating premise."
*–Booklist*

Hard COVER PAPER BACK

Date Read: ________ My Rating (circle): ★ ★ ★ ★ ★

My Comments: ________

# Conflict of Interest
## by Terry Lewis

Want to Read

*1997 • Pineapple Press, Inc. • 328 pages*

**Setting:** Tallahassee, Florida, 1990s
**Type:** Criminal defense attorney

Ted Stevens is suffering through a divorce and has a serious alcohol problem. When he is appointed to defend Bobby Jackson, who is accused of murdering his lover Patty Stiles, he has a chance to get back on his feet. However, Patty was Ted's mistress as well. He soon finds himself torn between self-preservation and the defense of his client when evidence surfaces that could exonerate his client, but would incriminate Ted himself. Worst of all, because of an alcohol-induced blackout, Ted has no idea what he really was doing on the night of the murder. Will this conflict of interest keep justice from prevailing?

"This well-crafted drama rings with authenticity all the way to its heart-stopping conclusion."
*–Publishers Weekly*

☐ Hard COVER ☐ PAPER BACK

☐ Date Read: ________ My Rating (circle): ★ ★ ★ ★ ★

My Comments: ____________________

# Angle of Impact
## by Bonnie MacDougal

☐ Want to Read

*1998 • Ballantine Books • 355 pages*

**Setting:** Philadelphia, 1990s
**Type:** Corporate attorney

In this novel inspired by actual events, attorney Dana Svenssen's life is dramatically changed when a helicopter carrying her biggest client collides with a small plane over the Philadelphia amusement park where

her two daughters are spending the day. The girls are unharmed, but the crash kills everyone on board the two aircrafts, as well as several people on the ground. When Dana becomes involved in the subsequent litigation and assembles a team of experts to reconstruct the disaster, it becomes chillingly apparent that someone doesn't want the truth revealed and that she and her family are in grave danger.

". . . a fast-paced ride . . ."
*–The Chicago Tribune*

☐ Hard COVER ☐ PAPER BACK ☐ Audio

☐ Date Read: ________ My Rating (circle): ★ ★ ★ ★ ★

My Comments: ______________________________

# Gone, but not Forgotten
## by Phillip Margolin

Want to Read

*1993 • Doubleday • 384 pages*

New York Times #12
1 Week On List

**Setting:** Portland, Oregon, 1990s
**Type:** Criminal defense attorney

A serial killer who tortures and mutilates the wives of prominent local businessmen is on the loose. The killer leaves behind a black rose and a note reading, "Gone, But Not Forgotten." In the midst of this, feminist defense attorney Betsy Tannenbaum is retained by millionaire Martin Darius for services that may be needed in the future. Soon after, several corpses are discovered on a construction site owned by Darius. Betsy must now discover the truth behind these murders that resemble crimes that occurred in New York 10 years ago – but the killer who had committed those crimes had supposedly been caught . . .

". . . a top-notch whodunit with an explosive and satisfying conclusion."
*–Publishers Weekly*

☐ Hard COVER ☐ PAPER BACK ☐ Audio

☐ Date Read: __________ My Rating (circle): ★ ★ ★ ★ ★

My Comments: ______________________________

# Compelling Evidence
## by Steve Martini

Want to Read

*1992 • G.P. Putnam's Sons • 384 pages*

**Setting:** California, 1990s
**Type:** Criminal defense attorney

Ben Potter, a successful lawyer who's about to be nominated for a seat on the Supreme Court, is found dead in his office, apparently a victim of suicide. But then it is discovered he was murdered, and his wife Talia is accused of the crime. Defense attorney Paul Madriani is thrust into Talia's defense by Potter's law partner Tony Skarpellos. Complicating matters is that Madriani had an affair a few years back with Talia, plus the fact that Skarpellos seemingly will inherit the profitable firm if Talia is indicted. Madriani's sure there's been a set-up, but to reveal the truth may be too risky for his own good.

***CheckerBee Note***

This is one of four books featuring attorney Paul Madriani.

☐ Hard COVER ☐ PAPER BACK ☐ LARGE PRINT ☐ Audio

☐ Date Read: ____________ My Rating (circle): ★ ★ ★ ★ ★

My Comments: ____________________________________________

# Face Value
## by Lia Matera

Want to Read

*1994 • Simon & Schuster • 221 pages*

**Setting:** California, 1990s
**Type:** Civil litigator

Attorney Laura Di Palma has just gone into private practice and she's ready to take any case that comes her way. Her first client is a former colleague who's gotten tangled up with a New Age guru named Brother Mike. Brother Mike has been videotaping his followers in compromising positions, then distributing the tapes. When Laura agrees to take the case, she doesn't realize how deeply it will draw her into the tawdry world of sex-for-sale, or that Brother Mike's shady dealings will leave her with a multiple-murder case on her hands.

***CheckerBee Note***

This is one of five books by Matera featuring attorney Laura Di Palma.

Hard COVER    PAPER BACK

Date Read: ________ My Rating (circle): ★ ★ ★ ★ ★

My Comments: ____________________

# The Tenth Justice
## by Brad Meltzer

Want to Read

*1997 • Rob Weisbach Books*
*400 pages*

New York Times #8
7 Weeks On List

**Setting:** Washington, D.C., 1990s
**Type:** Supreme Court law clerk

Ben Addison has just landed a prestigious position as a law clerk for a Supreme Court justice. However, things go wrong when he divulges a confidential decision that hasn't been made public yet and someone makes millions of dollars off the leak. Deciding not to go to the proper authorities, Ben instead turns to friends to make use of their political connections. But when there's a leak among the friends, their careers are put on the line and their lives in jeopardy.

"Meltzer spins a mean paranoid fantasy that'll have you turning pages in a frenzy."
*–Kirkus Reviews*

### CheckerBee Note

The film rights to this novel were sold to Fox 2000.

☐ Hard COVER ☐ PAPER BACK ☐ LARGE PRINT ☐ Audio

☐ Date Read: __________ My Rating (circle): ★ ★ ★ ★ ★

My Comments: ______________________________

# Rumpole of the Bailey
## by John Mortimer

Want to Read

*1978 • Penguin • 208 pages*

**Setting:** London, 1970s
**Type:** Barrister

In this collection of short stories, Horace Rumpole takes on clients from all ends of the social spectrum. He is one of those rare attorneys who relies on his quick British wit and his own moral code. Included in this collection (in alphabetical order) are: "Rumple and the Alternative Society," "Rumpole and the Heavy Brigade," "Rumpole and the Honorable Member," "Rumpole and the Learned Friends," "Rumpole and the Married Lady" and "Rumpole and the Younger Generation."

### CheckerBee Note

Horace Rumpole was featured on a British television series in the 1980s starring Leo McKern. The series later aired in the United States as part of the PBS *Mystery!* series. Episodes of the television series are now available on video.

☐ Hard COVER ☐ PAPER BACK ☐ LARGE PRINT ☐ Audio

☐ Date Read: ________ My Rating (circle): ★ ★ ★ ★ ★

My Comments: ____________________

# The Little Death
## by Michael Nava

Want to Read

*1986 • Alyson Publications, Inc. • 165 pages*

**Setting:** California, 1980s
**Type:** Criminal defense attorney

Henry Rios, a gay Latino attorney based in San Francisco, is contacted by Hugh Paris, a drug-addicted black sheep of a wealthy family who says that his grandfather, who disapproves of his lifestyle, is out to kill him. Henry doesn't believe him – that is, until Hugh actually does wind up dead, the victim of an apparent accident. But Henry knows that this death was no accident. The clues lead him directly to Hugh's family – a family full of old money and greed – and a terrible history of abuse and murder that Henry vows to expose.

***CheckerBee Note***

This is the first of six novels to feature Henry Rios.

PAPER BACK

Date Read: ________ My Rating (circle): ★ ★ ★ ★ ★

My Comments: ________

# Criminal Seduction
## by Darian North

Want to Read

*1993 • Dutton • 534 pages*

**Setting:** New York City and Stoatsberg, New York, 1990s
**Type:** Writer

Author Owen Byrne gets the chance to escape his family's midwestern home when his agent sends him to upstate New York to gather material about a trial for a true-crime book. The trial involves the murder of an internationally famous artist, Bram Serian by his Asian wife Lenore (dubbed by the press as the "Black Widow"). It seems like an open-and-shut case but Owen is not so sure. He delves deeper into the case and begins to explore Bram's enigmatic past as well as Lenore's. Is Lenore really innocent or is Owen blinded by his attraction to her?

"The characters are well drawn and interesting, the plot is twisted and supple . . . an absorbing first novel."
–*Booklist*

Hard COVER PAPER BACK

Date Read: ________ My Rating (circle): ★ ★ ★ ★ ★

My Comments: ________________

# Motion to Suppress
## by Perri O'Shaughnessy

Want to Read

*1995 • Delacorte Press • 432 pages*

**Setting:** Lake Tahoe, 1990s
**Type:** Criminal defense attorney

Attorney Nina Reilly has left her law practice and failed marriage behind in San Francisco and moved to Lake Tahoe seeking a fresh start. Barely settled in, she becomes entangled in a case involving a local waitress and her abusive husband. Misty, the accused waitress, remembers hitting her husband with a heavy object during an argument, but nothing after that. When her husband turns up at the bottom of a lake the next day, Misty is suspected. Nina reluctantly takes the case, not convinced that Misty is innocent, and sets out to find the killer, hoping that all roads won't lead to Misty.

### CheckerBee Note

"Perri O'Shaughnessy" is the pseudonym for sisters Mary and Pamela O'Shaughnessy

Hard COVER  PAPER BACK  LARGE PRINT  Audio

Date Read: ____________ My Rating (circle): ★ ★ ★ ★ ★

My Comments: ____________

# Suspicion of Innocence
## by Barbara Parker

☐ Want to Read

*1994 • Dutton • 343 pages*

**Setting:** Miami, 1990s
**Type:** Litigation attorney

Gail Connor, an attorney ascending in the ranks at a large Miami law firm, receives news that her sister Renee was found dead in the Everglades. Renee's wrists were slashed and the police initially ruled it a suicide. To make things worse, Gail's marriage begins to fall apart and when her sister's death is ruled a murder, Gail is the prime suspect. With the help of Anthony Quintana, Gail works to clear her name, while finding out the truth behind the life and death of the sister she never really knew.

"... an intelligently steamy first novel."
*–Kirkus Reviews*

☐ TV MOVIE *Sisters and Other Strangers* (1997) starring Debrah Farentino and Joanna Kerns

☐ Hard COVER ☐ PAPER BACK ☐ LARGE PRINT ☐ Audio

☐ Date Read: ________ My Rating (circle): ★ ★ ★ ★ ★

My Comments:

# The Lasko Tangent
## by Richard North Patterson

☐ Want to Read

*1979 • W.W. Norton & Company • 255 pages*

**Setting:** Washington, D.C and Boston, 1970s
**Type:** U.S. attorney

William Lasko always gets what he wants. He is a self-made millionaire with powerful connections, including the president himself. The Economic Crimes Commission knows Lasko's practices are corrupt and wants to expose him.

U.S. Attorney Christopher Paget is assigned this formidable task, but Lasko likes to eliminate his problems. Alexander Lehman is one such problem and minutes after he offers to talk to Paget, he is run down by a car. And that is just the beginning of what will be done to protect William Lasko.

### *Awards*

1980 Edgar Award winner for
Best First Novel by an American Author

☐ Hard COVER ☐ PAPER BACK ☐ Audio

☐ Date Read: ____________ My Rating (circle): ★ ★ ★ ★ ★

My Comments: ________________________________

________________________________

________________________________

________________________________

# Mitigating Circumstances
## by Nancy Taylor Rosenberg

☐ Want to Read

*1993 • Dutton • 362 pages*

**Setting:** California, 1990s
**Type:** Assistant district attorney

Lily Forrester is a successful assistant D.A. who has just been promoted to Chief of the Sex Crimes Division. Unfortunately, her marriage has not been so successful and is on the verge of collapse. Then tragedy strikes when an intruder breaks into her home, attacks Lily and rapes her 13-year-old daughter at knifepoint. Lily goes against the law she has always worked to uphold to assuage her own need for vengeance. She tracks down and shoots the attacker and carefully covers up the crime. Now she must cope with both the guilt of her vigilante actions and her terror of being discovered.

***CheckerBee Note***

The film rights to this novel were sold to Tri-Star Pictures.

☐ Hard COVER ☐ PAPER BACK ☐ LARGE PRINT ☐ Audio

☐ Date Read: ________ My Rating (circle): ★ ★ ★ ★ ★

My Comments: ________

# Final Appeal
## by Lisa Scottoline

☐ Want to Read

*1994 • HarperPaperbacks • 352 pages*

**Setting:** Philadelphia, 1990s
**Type:** Law clerk

When Philadelphia lawyer Grace Rossi takes a part-time job as a law clerk to make ends meet after her divorce, she doesn't expect to start a romance with a handsome judge who assigns her to a death penalty case.

When he turns up dead after an apparent suicide, Grace doesn't believe for a minute that he killed himself. She begins investigating his murder and turns up some very interesting evidence of corruption and bribery among some very powerful and influential people. But her knowledge of the truth will put her own life in danger.

". . . an exciting, action-packed read."
*–Publishers Weekly*

### Awards

1995 Edgar Award winner for Best Paperback Original

☐ PAPER BACK ☐ LARGE PRINT

☐ Date Read: ____________ My Rating (circle): ★ ★ ★ ★ ★

My Comments: ______________________________

# The Perfect Witness
## by Barry Siegel

Want to Read

*1998 • Ballantine Books • 352 pages*

**Setting:** La Graciosa, California, 1990s
**Type:** Criminal defense attorney

Idealistic and honest attorney Greg Monarch is about to face the biggest challenge of his career. When his friend and former partner Ira Sullivan is accused of murder, Greg agrees to defend him. But Greg is up against the prosecution's perfect witness: Sandy Polson, a beautiful charmer who claims to know Ira's guilty because she was with him the night of the murder and saw everything. Sandy's strength isn't honesty, but that doesn't concern the overly ambitious district attorney. Now Greg's only chance to win is to beat them at their own game, as an honest attorney must learn to play dirty to save his friend.

"... an intriguing blend of mystery, suspense, and courtroom drama ..."
*–Library Journal*

☐ Hard COVER ☐ PAPER BACK ☐ Audio

☐ Date Read: ____________ My Rating (circle): ★ ★ ★ ★ ★

My Comments: ____________

# Expert Testimony
## by Grif Stockley

Want to Read

*1991 • Summit Books • 285 pages*

**Setting:** Arkansas, 1990s
**Type:** Public defender

When the popular and powerful state senator, Hart Anderson, is shot and killed by Perry Sarver, public defender Gideon Page takes on the defense of Sarver, who was a psychiatric patient of Anderson's wife. There seems to be no way Gideon can win the case, the only option is the obvious insanity plea. Then, as Gideon dives further into the case, he uncovers more than he bargained for – secrets that make his open-and-shut insanity case something different all together.

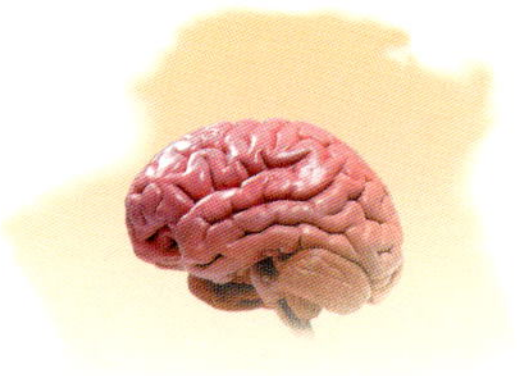

"The strengths of this uncontrived first novel lie in Stockley's thorough legal knowledge and a fluent writing style marked by humor and insight."
*–Publishers Weekly*

☐ Hard COVER ☐ PAPER BACK ☐ Audio

☐ Date Read: ________ My Rating (circle): ★ ★ ★ ★ ★

My Comments: ____________________

# No Lesser Plea
## by Robert K. Tanenbaum

☐ Want to Read

*1987 • Franklin Watts • 316 pages*

**Setting:** New York City, 1970s
**Type:** Assistant district attorney

Butch Karp, an ex-basketball jock who's now an assistant D.A., is prosecuting accused murderer Mandeville Louis. Butch has strong ideals of the justice system and he's determined to win. Louis, however, has other ideas. He conveniently feigns insanity to avoid trial and stay out of jail. While Butch is matching wits with the equally determined Louis and his attorney, he's also trying to learn to deal with the political maneuverings of the D.A.'s office, his wacky coworkers and his crumbling belief in a justice system he once thought worked.

". . . Tanenbaum has infused this book with a strong collection of characters . . . [and] a raunchy energy that crackles in the out-of-office lawyer talk."
*–Publishers Weekly*

☐ Hard COVER ☐ PAPER BACK

☐ Date Read: ________ My Rating (circle): ★ ★ ★ ★ ★

My Comments: ________

# The Codicil
## by Tom Topor

Want to Read

*1995 • Hyperion • 338 pages*

**Setting:** New York City, 1990s
**Type:** Private detective

Millionaire Matthew Marshall dies, leaving his wife and three children to inherit his $105-million estate. But the family is shocked to discover that Marshall added a codicil to his will that grants half of the estate to a previously unacknowledged child he had during his service in Vietnam. Marshall's estate hires Adam Bruno, a street-smart former defense attorney, to locate the child. Just as the case begins to look hopeless, Bruno begins to uncover some secrets – secrets that may prove quite dangerous.

"Topor builds excruciating tension in this page-turner, with rock solid plotting leading readers through a maze of shocking surprises few will see coming."
*–Publishers Weekly*

Hard COVER | PAPER BACK | LARGE PRINT | Audio

Date Read: ______ My Rating (circle): ★ ★ ★ ★ ★

My Comments:

# Anatomy of a Murder
## by Robert Traver

☐ Want to Read

*1958 • St. Martin's Press*
*437 pages*

New York Times #1
59 Weeks On List

**Setting:** Iron Cliffs, Michigan, 1950s
**Type:** Criminal defense attorney

Paul Biegler had just been replaced as Iron Cliffs County's D.A. – a job he loved. So when Laura Manion asks him to defend her husband in a murder case, he can't refuse the chance to prove himself – this time on the side of the defense. Manion had shot local barkeep Barney Quill after he found out Quill had raped Laura. Biegler decides to make a temporary insanity plea for his client, as he makes a detailed study into the anatomy of a murder, discovering more than he bargained for.

"It held me as few books have,
I couldn't put it down."
*–New York Times Book Review*

☐ MOVIE (1959) starring James Stewart, Lee Remick, Ben Gazzara and George C. Scott

☐ Hard COVER ☐ PAPER BACK ☐ LARGE PRINT ☐ Audio ☐ Video

☐ Date Read: ____________ My Rating (circle): ★ ★ ★ ★ ★

My Comments: ____________________________________________

# Presumed Innocent
## by Scott Turow

Want to Read

*1987 • Farrar, Straus and Giroux*
*431 pages*

New York Times #1
44 Weeks On List

**Setting:** Kindle County, 1980s
**Type:** Chief deputy prosecuting attorney

Carolyn Polhemus, a prosecuting attorney in Kindle County, has been found raped and murdered. Her colleague Rusty Sabich, with whom Carolyn had a secret affair, is put in charge of the investigation, and he needs to solve the case quickly – he's under pressure from his boss, who is in the midst of a reelection campaign. Unfortunately, the investigation is a disaster and everything starts to fall apart for Rusty. His relationship with Carolyn is revealed, and when a political enemy charges him with her murder, Rusty now finds *himself* on trial.

### Awards

1987 Silver Dagger Award winner
from the Crime Writers Association

MOVIE (1990) starring Harrison Ford and Brian Dennehy

Hard COVER  PAPER BACK  LARGE PRINT  Audio  Video

Date Read: ________ My Rating (circle): ★ ★ ★ ★ ★

My Comments:

# Mean Streak
## by Carolyn Wheat

☐ Want to Read

*1996 • Berkley Prime Crime • 236 pages*

**Setting:** New York City, 1990s
**Type:** Criminal defense attorney

Cass Jameson has agreed to defend her ex-lover, mob attorney Matt Riordan, against charges of bribery. Even though he left her for a younger woman and broke her heart, she cannot believe that he is guilty of bribing a court clerk for the grand jury. Things begin to look bleak as the prosecution's witnesses say just the right things. And they look even bleaker when those same witnesses begin turning up dead. Although the deaths almost guarantee a mistrial

for Matt, he may now be charged with murder. Cass must convince herself that Matt is not responsible and clear his name before it's too late.

"Exuding a love of New York and building to a fine finish, this is probably Wheat's best novel."
*–Armchair Detective*

☐ Hard COVER ☐ PAPER BACK

☐ Date Read: ______ My Rating (circle): ★ ★ ★ ★ ★

My Comments: ______

# Death Qualified
## by Kate Wilhelm

☐ Want to Read

*1991 • St. Martin's Press • 438 pages*

**Setting:** Oregon, 1980s
**Type:** Criminal defense attorney

Disillusioned with the justice system, Barbara Holloway gave up practicing law five years ago. Now, her father urges her to take the difficult case of Nell Kendricks, who is accused of killing her husband Lucas. Lucas deserted his family seven years ago to take part in a top-secret research study on the chaos theory. He wasn't heard from until the day he came back to Oregon and wound up dead. Now it's up to Barbara to save Nell, and to do so, she must discover the connection between Lucas' death, some computer disks and his mysterious project.

"Another heaven-storming hybrid of mystery and fantasy from veteran Wilhelm . . ."
*–Kirkus Reviews*

☐ Hard COVER ☐ PAPER BACK

☐ Date Read: ______________ My Rating (circle): ★ ★ ★ ★ ★

My Comments: ______________________________

# The Deal
## by Sabin Willett

Want to Read

*1996 • Random House • 448 pages*

**Setting:** Boston, 1992
**Type:** Corporate attorney

The law firm of Freer, Motley & Stone has just completed an $840 million deal. However, a paperwork error was overlooked and the amount was changed to $840,000. Now the law firm could be held liable and owe millions. When a senior partner winds up dead, the blame of the paperwork change and the murder falls on John Shepard, who was known to be bitter after not making partner. John calls in a favor from Ed Mulcahy, an in-house litigator who's out of practice with criminal law, who agrees to defend him. Ed can only hope to argue that John was framed by another lawyer at the firm. But who and why?

"Willett, a debut novelist, impressively maintains the suspense and convincingly conveys courtroom atmosphere."
*–Booklist*

☐ Hard COVER ☐ PAPER BACK ☐ Audio

☐ Date Read: ____________ My Rating (circle): ★ ★ ★ ★ ★

My Comments: ____________

# Dead in the Water
## by Stuart Woods

☐ Want to Read

*1997 • HarperCollins • 325 pages*

**Setting:** St. Marks, 1990s
**Type:** Criminal defense attorney

When Allison Manning sails into St. Marks without her husband, millionaire author Paul Manning, she explains that he died of a heart attack while they were at sea, and that she had to throw his body overboard. The island's minister of justice, Sir Winston Sutherland, who could use a successful murder case to aid him in becoming the island's next prime minister, is suspicious and charges Allison with murder. Vacationing attorney Stone Barrington, who can't resist a beautiful maiden in distress, takes up her cause with relish, even when it begins to look like she's guilty. Can he see past his attraction to get to the truth?

". . . a cleverly plotted, witty crime caper . . ."
*–Booklist*

☐ Hard COVER ☐ PAPER BACK ☐ LARGE PRINT ☐ Audio

☐ Date Read: ____________ My Rating (circle): ★ ★ ★ ★ ★

My Comments: ____________

# About The Authors

Most of the authors featured in this checklist are best-selling legal thriller authors with many popular titles to their credit. If you enjoyed the book in the checklist, head to your local bookstore or library to find other titles by the same author. In this section, we give you biographical glimpses of each featured author.

**David Baldacci** served as a Washington, D.C. corporate and trial lawyer for many years after graduating from the University of Virginia School of Law. After leaving the profession to write full-time, he published the well-known novels *The Winner*, *The Simple Truth* and *Total Control*. *Absolute Power*, his debut novel, became a motion picture directed by Clint Eastwood.

**William Bernhardt** began his writing career with the novel *Primary Justice*, which went on to become a best seller and launched the popular "Justice" series starring attorney Ben Kincaid. Bernhardt, a graduate of the University of Oklahoma College of Law, was named one of the top 25 young lawyers in the nation and has earned an Oklahoma Book Award for his writing.

**Bill Blum** is a an administrative law judge, who also served as an attorney on two of California's death row trial appeals. Adding to his writing resume are numerous articles in various publications including *ABA Journal*, *California Lawyer* and *The Los Angeles Times*.

## About The Authors

**Jay Brandon** began his writing career while still in law school and his first book was published in 1985, the year he graduated. He has had a successful law career working in Bexar County's District Attorney's office and sitting on the Texas Court of Criminal Appeals. His first courtroom novel, *Fade the Heat* (1990) was nominated for an Edgar Award for Best Novel. His other books include *Angel of Death* and *Rules of Evidence.*

**D.W. Buffa** received his doctorate in political science from the University of Chicago and then went on to serve as an Oregon defense attorney for 10 years. Buffa has followed up his 1997 best-selling debut novel *The Defense* with *The Prosecution.*

**Sarah Caudwell** is the pseudonym of Sarah Cockburn, who studied law at Oxford. London's Lincoln Inn, the setting for much of *Thus Was Adonis Murdered,* is where she practiced law for several years. She is the author of two other novels featuring Hilary Tamar, *The Shortest Way to Hades* and *The Sirens Sang of Murder,* which won the Anthony Award for Best Novel in 1990.

**William J. Coughlin** served as both a prosecutor and defense attorney, as well as a federal judge. In his lifetime, Coughlin published over 10 novels including *Her Honor* and *The Twelve Apostles.* Coughlin's losing battle with cancer is chronicled in his wife, Ruth's, 1993 book *Grieving.*

**Robert Daley** is a former deputy New York Police Department commissioner, whose writing career includes a stint as a *New York Times* correspondent. His works include the critically acclaimed *A Faint Cold Fear* and *The Dangerous Edge*. Several of his novels have been adapted into movies.

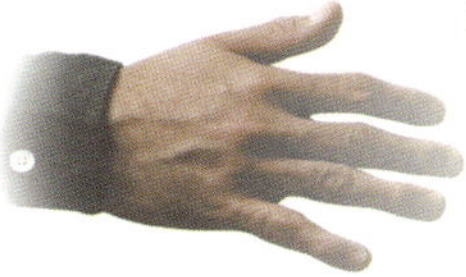

Best-selling author **William Diehl** is the author of two other novels featuring defense attorney Martin Vail: *Show of Evil* (1995) and *Reign in Hell* (1997). He is the author of several other thrillers as well, including *27, Sharky's Machine* and *Thai Horse.*

**Richard Dooling** earned his law degree from St. Louis University in Missouri. He was a successful attorney with the St. Louis firm Bryan Cave, but left in 1991 to pursue his writing career. Dooling is the author of several novels including *White Man's Grave*, which was a finalist for the 1994 National Book Award. He is also a frequent contributor to *The New Yorker, The New York Times* and the *National Law Journal.*

**Michael C. Eberhardt** practices as a criminal defense attorney. His first novel, *Body of a Crime*, is based on the famous "no body" murder trial, his winning case that boasts being the longest murder trial that resulted in acquittal in U.S. history. He is also the author of *Against the Law.*

**Linda Fairstein** received her degree in law from the University of Virginia School of Law. For over 20 years, she has run the Manhattan's District Attorney's office Sex

Crimes Unit. In addition to her fictional work, Fairstein has published the nonfiction title, *Sexual Violence: Our War Against Rape*, which in 1994, was named a *New York Times* notable book. In 1993, she was named "Woman of the Year" by both *New Woman* and *Glamour*.

**Joy Fielding** claims to have gotten an early start as a writer when she sent her first story to a magazine at 8 years old. She spent her childhood writing plays that she and her friends acted out and even wrote a script for TV when she was 12. Fielding graduated from the University of Toronto with a B.A. in English literature, and it was then that she decided to pursue acting. Eventually, Fielding turned her full attention back to writing and has since published over 10 novels.

**Joseph Finder** studied at the Yale and Harvard Russian Research Center. He has taught at Harvard as well. Finder's writing credits include *The Moscow Club* and *The Zero Hour*, and he has also contributed to *The New Republic, The New York Times* and *The Washington Post*.

**J.F. Freedman** made his debut in the world of fiction in 1991 with *Against The Wind*. He began his career as a writer and director for both television and motion pictures. He is the author of several novels including *The Disappearance* and *Key Witness*.

**Philip Friedman** is an accomplished attorney as well as a writer. His other works include the best-selling *Inadmissible Evidence, Grand Jury* and *Rage*, which was made into a movie starring George C. Scott.

**Ira Genberg** is a well-respected and successful trial attorney. *Reckless Homicide* marks his debut into the world of fiction and was nominated for a 1999 Edgar Award. The success of this debut novel leaves readers anxiously anticipating Genberg's next work.

**James Grippando**, a partner at Florida's Seel Hector & Davis is also a trial lawyer. He made his literary debut with *The Pardon*, but claims that his real first novel is one that sits on a closet shelf, never having been published. Grippando has also written *The Abduction*, *The Informant* and *Found Money*.

**John Grisham** is one of the most famous and successful writers of the modern legal thriller. Grisham received his undergraduate degree in accounting from Mississippi State University and his law degree from the University of Mississippi. Grisham practiced criminal and civil law and was elected to the Mississippi House of Representatives. All of his books have been best sellers and many have been made into blockbuster feature films.

## About The Authors

**Gini Hartzmark** attended both the business and law schools of the University of Chicago, but decided that her true love was writing. She was a business and economics writer and has contributed many articles to Chicago newspapers and national magazines. Hartzmark is the author of the popular Kate Millholland series, which includes *Principal Defense* (which was nominated for the 1993 Edgar Award for Best Paperback Original).

**Michael A. Kahn** received his law degree from Harvard University and has enjoyed a successful career as a trial lawyer in a prominent firm. He has published a series of novels featuring Rachel Gold, an attorney whose life often mirrors is own.

**John Katzenbach**, once a criminal court reporter, is the author of several novels including *In the Heat of the Summer* and *The Shadow Man*, which were both nominated for an Edgar Award. Aside from his successful career in fiction, Katzenbach's writing experience includes contributions to *The Miami Herald*, the *Miami News* and *Herald's Tropic* magazine.

**Lelia Kelly**, born in Atlanta, began her professional career as a banker. However, she turned to writing and *Presumption of Guilt*, her debut novel, has catapulted Kelly into the legal thriller spotlight with its rave reviews.

Since **John T. Lescroart's** literary debut, his works have been critically acclaimed, including receiving nominations for Shamus and Anthony awards. One characteristic of Lescroart's writing is that his characters often appear throughout several novels. Aside from writing, the author has a passion for gourmet cooking.

**Paul Levine** received his undergraduate degree in journalism from Penn State and his first job was as a reporter for *The Miami Herald*. After graduating from the University of Miami Law School, Levine practiced civil litigation during which he became well-known for his knowledge of First Amendment issues. When he turned to writing, he introduced the popular Jake Lassiter series. He also wrote the syndicated television show *You Be The Judge* (with other television projects on the way) and a nationally syndicated column.

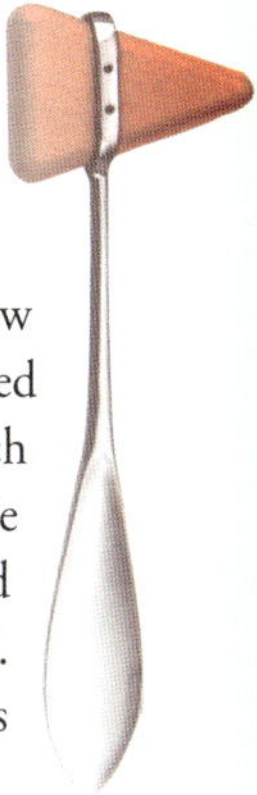

**Harry Levy** is a preventative-medicine specialist who has studied at Columbia, New York University and Yale. As an intern, he directed an acclaimed documentary *Interned*, which documented his experiences during that year. He is also the executive editor of a web site dedicated to health professionals called Cyberounds©. *Chain of Custody* is his first book and utilizes this medical knowledge.

**Terry Lewis**, a trial judge, claims that writing is just his hobby. When not in court or writing, much of his focus is on law education for established judges as well as for children. *Conflict of Interest* is his first novel.

## About The Authors

Native Philadelphian **Bonnie MacDougal** is a University of Pennsylvania Law School graduate, and was a trial attorney for 16 years. She claims that she only began writing seriously about six years ago and when *Breach of Trust* was published, she left her legal career. *Angle of Impact* was inspired by actual cases in which she was involved. Although MacDougal is now a full-time author, she frequently works as a legal consultant.

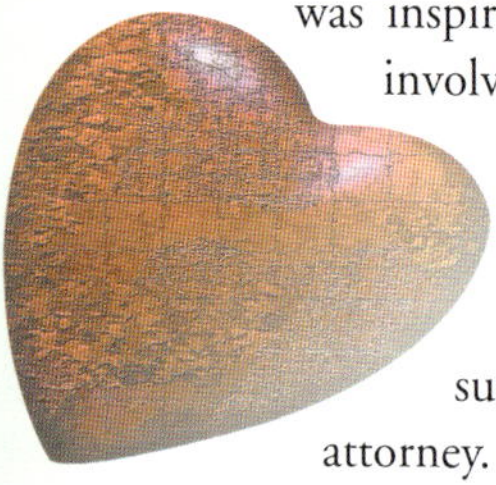

**Phillip Margolin** has been as successful a writer as he has a defense attorney. His novels have consistently reached the top of the best-seller charts. Margolin is well-known for his many high-profile murder cases as well as being the first attorney in Oregon to use the battered woman's syndrome defense in a murder case.

**Steve Martini**, as a trial attorney and state attorney, has served both the public and private sectors of law. Martini has also been a journalist and a capital correspondent in the California State House in Sacramento for the *Los Angeles Daily Journal.* In addition to *Compelling Evidence*, he has written several other Paul Madriani books.

**Lia Matera** graduated from Hastings College of Law, and then went on to work as a teaching fellow at Stanford Law School. Her works, including her novels featuring Laura Di Palma, have won her numerous praises, including nominations for Anthony and Edgar Awards.

**Brad Meltzer** made his debut into the literary world with his novel, *The Tenth Justice.* After graduating from Columbia Law School, he worked in the marketing department at *Games* magazine and wrote speeches for President Clinton's national service program.

**John Mortimer** is an English author and dramatist who has written both for the stage and for television. He was once, like his popular character Rumpole, a barrister, and many see Rumpole as Mortimer's alter ego. His extensive writing credits include several novels, plays and an autobiography.

**Michael Nava** received his law degree at Stanford University after studying at Colorado College on a full scholarship, and spending a year in Argentina on a fellowship. He then served as both a Los Angeles deputy city attorney and a research attorney for the California Court of Appeals. Nava has won numerous Lambda Literary Awards for his series about Henry Rios, a gay Latino attorney in California.

**Darian North's** works have earned her much praise, including an Edgar Award nomination. She is the author of several thrillers including *Violation* and *Thief of Souls.* While writing is her passion, her four children are the center of her life, and *Thief of Souls* has been dedicated to them.

## About The Authors

**Perri O'Shaughnessy** is the combined pseudonym for sisters Mary and Pamela O'Shaughnessy. Mary is a University of California graduate who became a writer and editor after graduation. Pamela is a Harvard Law School graduate who was a trial lawyer for 16 years. Their character Nina Reilly is featured in several novels.

**Barbara Parker** worked as a prosecutor for the Dade County State Attorney's Office before going into private practice. Then she stepped away from her legal career and obtained a master's degree in creative writing. Her works have been praised, including her novels featuring character Gail Connor.

Edgar Award-winning author **Richard North Patterson** received an undergraduate degree from Ohio Wesleyan University and his law degree from Case Western Reserve University. His law experience includes service in the Ohio Attorney General Office and a trial lawyer for the U.S. Securities and Exchange Commission. Patterson later studied creative writing at the University of Alabama.

**Nancy Taylor Rosenberg** majored in English at Gulf Park College. She then spent more than 10 years in law enforcement both as a policewoman and a investigative probation officer. Rosenberg began writing her first novel, *Mitigating Circumstances*, after becoming bedridden due to a horse riding accident. Rosenberg participates in many charitable endeavors including her writing program for inner-city children and in 1995, she was voted "Woman of the Year" by the Boy Scouts of America.

**Lisa Scottoline** earned a B.A. in English and a law degree from the University of Pennsylvania Law School. Her legal thrillers are based upon her experiences as a lawyer at a Philadelphia law firm and her federal and state clerkships. Scottoline has also served as a visiting professor and lecturer on legal ethics at law schools around the United States. Her writing has been critically acclaimed.

**Barry Siegel** is an award-winning *Los Angeles Times* reporter. Known for his nonfiction books, one of which, *A Death in White Bear Lake*, was nominated for an Edgar Award in the Best Fact Crime category. *The Perfect Witness* catapulted him into the legal thriller genre and readers are eagerly awaiting his upcoming works of fiction.

**Grif Stockley** graduated from Rhodes College in Memphis. He has been an attorney for Central Arkansas Legal Services, which provides civil representation for the poor, and is also an adjunct professor at the University of Arkansas at Little Rock Law School. Stockley's character Gideon Page appears throughout his novels.

**Robert K. Tanenbaum** is the author of several novels featuring Butch Karp and Marlene Ciampi and has also authored nonfiction works. He is a former assistant district attorney and was appointed deputy chief counsel in investigating the assassinations of John F. Kennedy and Martin Luther King, Jr. Tanenbaum also worked as a special prosecutor consultant in the Hillside Strangler case.

**Tom Topor** has written in such genres as journalism and playwriting. He wrote the screenplay for the movie *The Accused*, as well as the script for the Broadway play *Nuts*, which was turned into a major motion picture. Topor also adds "novelist" to his resume, including the works *Coda* and *Bloodstar*.

**Robert Traver** is the pseudonym for John Donaldson Voelker. He went on to a long law career, including service as a prosecuting attorney and Michigan Supreme Court Justice. Traver is not only known for his legal expertise, but also his extensive knowledge of trout fishing.

Lawyer **Scott Turow's** writing career took off with the success of *Presumed Innocent*, and his subsequent novels have fared just as well. The Harvard Law graduate always harbored ambitions of becoming a novelist, and in fact received a fellowship to Stanford University's Creative Writing Center and taught creative writing at Stanford for several years before attending Harvard. Turow's legal credits include a partnership in an international law firm and criminal litigation.

**Carolyn Wheat** spent over two decades in the law profession as a defense attorney. She is the author of the popular Cass Jameson series which includes *Dead Man's Thoughts*, which was nominated for an Edgar Award. Wheat has written many short stories which have received numerous honors.

**Kate Wilhelm** is a multiple award-winning author whose works span genres. A prolific writer, her books have won Nebula, Hugo, Prix Apollo and Jupiter Awards. Wilhelm's works also include numerous short stories, which have received much praise as well.

**Sabin Willett** graduated from both Harvard and Harvard Law School. His legal experience includes a partnership with the prominent Boston law firm Bingham, Dana & Gould. Willett's debut novel *The Deal* has met with a great amount of praise, leaving his fans anxiously awaiting his next published work.

**Stuart Woods** is a bestselling author who pens the Stone Barrington series of books that also includes *Dirt* and *New York Dead*. After college, he held jobs in the field of advertising, but was finally able to turn his attention to his writing. With his 20 novels, Woods has received numerous honors, including an Edgar Award.

# Legal Thriller Book Awards

The following is an explanation of some of the prominent book awards given to legal thrillers and legal thriller novelists. As most legal thrillers involve crime, intrigue and discovery, they are most often categorized in the broader "mystery" genre. The awards are listed alphabetically according to the sponsoring organization.

## Bouchercon

**Anthony Award:** "Bouchercon," or "World Mystery Convention," is a convention that annually bestows the Anthony Award for Best Mystery Novel, Best First Mystery Novel, Best Paperback Original, Best Short Story and the like. The award is named after Anthony Boucher (a pseudonym for William Anthony Parker White), a prolific writer and supporter of mysterious fiction in the mid-20th century.

## Crime Writers Association

**Dagger Awards:** These awards are bestowed annually by the British-based Crime Writers Association. An independent committee picks the best crime novel of the year, as well as a runner-up. The Gold Dagger Award goes to the best novel, and the Silver Dagger Award to the runner-up. There is also a Last Laugh Dagger Award, given to the "most amusing" crime novel of the year. The Crime Writers Association also awards a Diamond Dagger in honor of a particular author's lifetime achievement in the field of mystery writing.

## Lambda Literary Foundation

**Lambda Literary Award:** These awards honor authors in the genres of gay and lesbian literature. There are numerous categories recognized by this organization, including Best Mystery.

## Malice Domestic Ltd.

**Agatha Award:** The Malice Domestic Mystery Convention is an annual gathering of fans of the traditional mystery. Their Agatha Award is awarded to any writer who emulates the traditional British cozy, a mystery popularized by Agatha Christie (for whom the award is named). Those attending vote on the various nominees.

## Mystery Readers International

**Macavity Award:** Each year, the Mystery Readers International membership votes on books published the previous year. The categories include Best Mystery Novel and Best First Mystery Novel. As its name suggests, Mystery Readers International is not so much a professional organization as a collection of readers. They publish *The Mystery Readers Journal.*

## Mystery Writers of America

**Edgar Award:** Named in honor of Edgar Allan Poe, who is regarded as the first mystery writer, the Edgar Award is conferred each year by the Mystery Writers of America. The recipient of the award must be a writer of mystery fiction published in the United States. The nominees are voted on by a closed committee and prizes are awarded for Best Novel and Best First Novel, among others. Founded in 1945, the Mystery Writers of America is an organization aimed at promoting and supporting authors, editors and publishers of mystery fiction.

**Grand Master Award:** The Mystery Writers of America also grants an annual award for an author's lifetime achievement in mystery fiction.

## Private Eye Writers of America

**Shamus Awards:** This prize is awarded annually by the Private Eye Writers of America. It honors writers of the private detective genre of mystery fiction, stories whose main characters are not professional investigators for the government, but private detectives. The categories include Best Private Eye Novel, Best First Private Eye Novel and Best Private Eye Short Story. In addition to the Shamus Awards, they have an Eye Award for lifetime achievement.

# Legal Glossary

**Accessory** – One who aids or contributes to a crime without being a key factor or who knowingly aids or hides a criminal.

**Accomplice** – A participant in the planning or execution of a crime.

**Acquittal** – A decision in a criminal court that finds the defendant not guilty.

**Admissible evidence** – Evidence in a civil or criminal trial that can be legally introduced.

**Affidavit** – A written statement made under oath to an officer of the court.

**Allegation** – A statement of fact, which a person will try to prove in court.

**Appeal** – A request made to a higher court to review the decision of a lower court.

**Arraignment** – The hearing at which an accused person is brought before the court to enter a plea to the criminal charge in the indictment.

**Assault** – The intentional attempt to inflict physical or verbal injury on someone.

**Bailiff** – A court officer whose duties include keeping order and maintaining proper courtroom etiquette.

**Bar** – Collective term for those licensed to practice law.

**Barrister** – A British lawyer.

**Battery** – A beating or other physical violence inflicted on another.

**Bench** – Specifically, the seat occupied by the judge; generally, the term can be applied to the court itself.

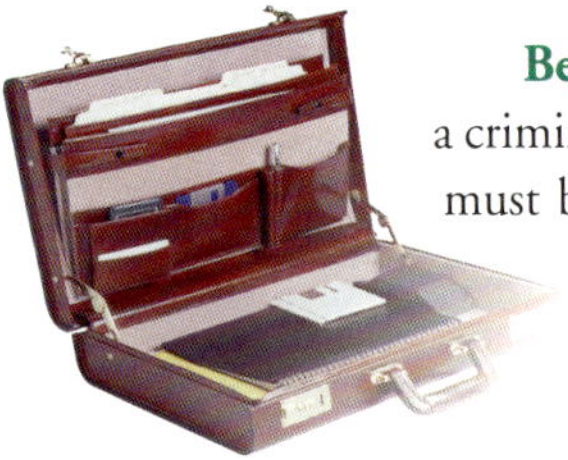

**Beyond a reasonable doubt** – In a criminal case, this means that the jury must be satisfied to a moral certainty that every element of the crime has been proven by the prosecution.

**Brief** – A document written by counsel of a case which summarizes the facts of a case, includes pertinent laws and explains how the law applies to the case.

**Burden of proof** – The necessity of the prosecution in a case to show that the defendant is guilty.

**Capital crime** – A crime that may be punishable by death.

**Circumstantial evidence** – Indirect proof that is deduced from other evidence or circumstances.

**Civil action** – An action which is brought before the court in order to protect private rights.

**Class action** – A lawsuit brought by one or more people on behalf of a larger group.

**Codicil** – An amendment or addition to a will.

**Contempt of court** – Disrupting the court by disobeying the commands of a judge or court order.

**Corporate law** – business law.

**Court martial** – A military court set up to try members of the armed forces and others within their jurisdiction.

**Cross examination** – Questioning of a witness by the opposite party, aimed at discrediting testimony.

**Defendant** – The person against whom a suit has been brought.

**Deposition** – The testimony of a witness or party that is taken under oath, but outside the courtroom.

**Disbarment** – A form of discipline that results in an attorney losing the right to practice law.

**District attorney** – A prosecutor who represents a judicial district and who prosecutes the crimes occurring in the district.

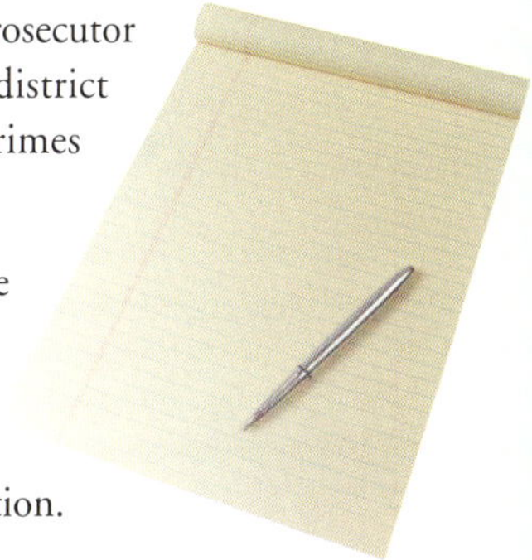

**Double jeopardy** – The practice of trying the same person twice for the same crime, a practice forbidden by the United States Constitution.

**Exhibit** – An item that is introduced as evidence during a trial or hearing.

**Felony** – Any offense, more serious than a misdemeanor, that is punishable by death or imprisonment for more than one year.

**Grand jury** – A jury who hears complaints and accusations in criminal matters, and who has the power to issue a formal indictment.

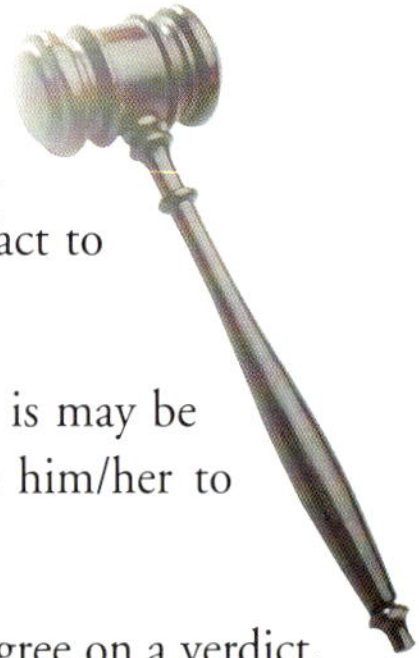

**Hearing** – A preliminary court proceeding that is usually less formal than a trial, but with issues of law or fact to be heard.

**Hostile witness** – A witness who is may be prejudiced against the party that calls him/her to the stand.

**Hung jury** – A jury that cannot agree on a verdict.

**Immunity** – A court assurance that someone will not face criminal charges in exchange for providing evidence.

**Indictment** – A written statement by a prosecuting authority charging someone with a crime.

**Jury** – A group of individuals sworn to give a verdict according to the evidence.

**Law clerk** – An assistant to a lawyer or a judge who does legal research and other tasks.

**Litigate** – To bring an action to a court of law.

**Malpractice** – Professional misconduct.

**Manslaughter** – The killing of a human being without premeditation or malice.

**Misdemeanor** – A lesser offense than a felony, and one that is usually punishable by fine or a prison term that is not served in a penitentiary.

**Mistrial** – A trial that becomes invalid because of a fundamental error and thus must begin again with the selection of a new jury.

**Mitigate** – To reduce or lessen.

**Murder** – The killing of a human being with deliberate intent. Murder in the first degree is a premeditated killing. Murder in the second degree is the sudden intent to kill without premeditation.

**Nolo contendere** – A plea offered by the defendant in a criminal action that announces his or her intention not to contest the action. The defendant is not admitting guilt but is still subject to conviction.

**Perjury** – Lying under oath. This is a criminal offense.

**Plaintiff** – The party filing a lawsuit.

**Plea** – The accused party's declaration of "guilty," "not guilty" or "nolo contendere."

**Plea bargain** – An agreement between the prosecutor and defendant that allows the defendant to plead guilty to a reduced charge.

**Preliminary hearing** – A hearing that is held so that a judge can decide whether or not a person charged with a crime should be put on trial.

**Pro bono** – Providing legal services for free.

## Legal Glossary

**Probable cause** – The reasonable belief that a crime has been committed and therefore the basis for all legal searches, seizures and arrests.

**Public defender** – A lawyer who provides free defense to an indigent person accused of a crime.

**Reasonable doubt** – A doubt that persists regarding the accused's guilt or innocence after evidence is presented. One cannot be convicted if there is reasonable doubt.

**Redirect examination** – After the cross examination, the party who called the witness can resume questioning.

**Stay** – An order by the court that stops a proceeding.

**Suborn** – To persuade to commit perjury or to obtain perjured testimony from a witness.

**Subpoena** – A legal document commanding a person to provide testimony at an appointed time and place.

**Testimony** – The evidence a witness gives under oath.

**Verdict** – A conclusion, by the jury, pertaining to fact or law from which the court forms a judgment.

**With prejudice** – A declaration or judgment dismissing all rights to bring or keep an action on the same claim.

**Without prejudice** – A declaration that a party has not lost any rights or privileges, and that they may bring a subsequent suit on the same claim.

# CheckerBee Checklist™

# Lawyer Type

This section lists the 50 featured legal thrillers according to type of lawyer the main protaganist is. This is a great way to keep track of which books you have read in each category – and which books you want to read.

## Assistant District Attorney

- ❑ *Final Jeopardy,* Linda Fairstein
- ❑ *Mitigating Circumstances,* Nancy Taylor Rosenberg
- ❑ *No Lesser Plea,* Robert K. Tanenbaum
- ❑ *Tainted Evidence,* Robert Daley

## Barrister

- ❑ *Rumpole of the Bailey,* John Mortimer
- ❑ *Thus Was Adonis Murdered,* Sarah Caudwell

## Chief Deputy Prosecuting Attorney

- ❑ *Presumed Innocent,* Scott Turow

## Civil Litigator

- ❑ *Face Value,* Lia Matera
- ❑ *Sheer Gall,* Michael A. Kahn

## Corporate Attorney

- ❏ *Absolute Power,* David Baldacci
- ❏ *Angle of Impact,* Bonnie MacDougal
- ❏ *The Deal,* Sabin Willett
- ❏ *Fatal Reaction,* Gini Hartzmark
- ❏ *The Firm,* John Grisham
- ❏ *Reckless Homicide,* Ira Genberg

## Criminal Defense Attorney

- ❏ *The 13th Juror,* John T. Lescroart
- ❏ *Against the Wind,* J.F. Freedman
- ❏ *Anatomy of a Murder,* Robert Traver
- ❏ *Compelling Evidence,* Steve Martini
- ❏ *Conflict of Interest,* Terry Lewis
- ❏ *Dead in the Water,* Stuart Woods
- ❏ *Death Qualified,* Kate Wilhelm
- ❏ *The Defense,* D.W. Buffa
- ❏ *Gone, but not Forgotten,* Phillip Margolin
- ❏ *High Crimes,* Joseph Finder
- ❏ *The Little Death,* Michael Nava
- ❏ *Local Rules,* Jay Brandon

## Criminal Defense Attorney, cont.

- ❑ *Mean Streak,* Carolyn Wheat
- ❑ *Motion to Suppress,* Perri O'Shaughnessy
- ❑ *The Pardon,* James Grippando
- ❑ *Perfect Justice,* William Bernhardt
- ❑ *The Perfect Witness,* Barry Siegel
- ❑ *Prejudicial Error,* Bill Blum
- ❑ *Presumption of Guilt,* Lelia Kelly
- ❑ *Primal Fear,* William Diehl
- ❑ *Reasonable Doubt,* Philip Friedman
- ❑ *Shadow of a Doubt,* William J. Coughlin

## District Attorney

- ❑ *Tell Me No Secrets,* Joy Fielding

## Law Clerk

- ❑ *Final Appeal,* Lisa Scottoline

## Law Student

- ❑ *Hart's War,* John Katzenbach

## Legal Researcher

- ❑ *Brain Storm,* Richard Dooling

## Litigation Attorney

- ❑ *Suspicion of Innocence,* Barbara Parker

## Medical Malpractice Litigator

- ❑ *Chain of Custody,* Harry Levy

## Private Detective

- ❑ *The Codicil,* Tom Topor

## Public Defender

- ❑ *Expert Testimony,* Grif Stockley
- ❑ *Witness for the Defense,* Michael C. Eberhardt

## Special Prosecutor

- ❑ *Night Vision,* Paul Levine

## Supreme Court Law Clerk

- ❑ *The Tenth Justice,* Brad Meltzer

## U.S. Attorney

- ❑ *The Lasko Tangent,* Richard North Patterson

## Writer

- ❑ *Criminal Seduction,* Darian North

## My Favorite Bookstores/Libraries

## My Favorite Books

## Great Reading Web Sites

***www.checklist.com***

## My Reading List

## Books Borrowed/Books Loaned

# Notes